# DESTROY CAPITALISM

## Before it Destroys Us!

# SHAWN GILLICK

# Destroy Capitalism Before It Destroys Us!

**First Edition** Copyright © 2023

**Second Edition** Copyright © 2025

**By Shawn Gillick**

**All Rights Reserved.**

DESTROY CAPITALISM BEFORE IT DESTROYS US!

# Table of Contents

# INTRODUCTION: WHAT THIS BOOK IS ABOUT & WHO SHOULD READ IT

## UPDATE TO THE INTRODUCTION:

**Donald J. Trump won the November 2024 American presidential election.** He won the popular and electoral votes (the election) fair and square. Unlike the January 6th, 2021 Insurrection that took place during his temper tantrum that caused thousands of citizens to storm the U.S. Capitol building in treasonous protest of the 2020 presidential election, there was no need for Trump to claim that the November 2024 presidential election was stolen. Not this time.

The American people handed over the power of the presidency to a convicted felon and man who clearly told Americans that he "would be dictator on day one" of his next term. **It's now February 26, 2025 (five weeks after his inauguration).** Trump has not only transitioned into his second term as president, but he has performed what is being called a "coup d'état" by installing an UNELECTED billionaire as "an aid" to head a fake so-called **"department of government efficiency" (DOGE)**. During this five-week government takeover, Trump has set the stage for implementing "project 25" which is currently being written about and had been written about and well documented online in every form imaginable. Trump & Elon Musk are attempting to install either one of them (or maybe even both of them) as dictators of America.

That said, many of the issues I raised when writing this book are even more important now than ever before. Please continue reading now through the lens of a new understanding of American history. The next four years of current affairs and politics is going to be very, very interesting to say the least. Thanks again for purchasing and reading my book. Now, onto the original introduction....

America is at a proverbial fork in the road. We seem to be staring down the barrel of possible global fascism if we're not careful in the 2024 presidential election. Add to that the global crisis of climate change, we're living in some incredibly strange times. With so much distrust in the institutions that have made our fragile democracy possible, with so much existential anxiety and distrust among American citizens, it's time we take a close look at the root cause(s) of this malaise. I'm not here to write much about myself. I am here to write about the world that you and I find ourselves living in. We're currently living in an era where some people think global capitalism is a very questionable "economy" and one where everything is peaches and cream with a strong American economy conducting business as usual. We live in an era of dire political circumstances.

Fascism is becoming "fashionable" again and it seems the adage that history doesn't *necessarily repeat itself, but rhymes,* is certainly true. There's a dire need for a book of this sort to be written. I don't think I need to do too much research online to see if books of this nature have already been written and published. There are countless books that have been published by academics, public intellectuals, journalists, celebrities and other authors discussing similar topics. I'm simply shooting from the hip and writing what I think can be done by leaders and citizens of society.

If I end up adding to what's already been written or is currently being written or if I'm creating a niche category of non-fiction, then so be it. My philosophical need is a burning desire to help usher in the end of capitalism. That is the end goal of this project. Personally, I feel capitalism should be destroyed but that's just a general declaration. I'm here to write about why I think it should be destroyed. My hunch is that it ought to be wrapped up, winded down and put to rest before it ends up killing off every animal in the animal kingdom. This obviously would include us *Homo sapiens.* Capitalism should be destroyed before it destroys you and your family. That's why I've titled this book *Destroy Capitalism before it destroys us!*

As I write, anyone who's been paying any attention to world news headlines knows that fascism seems to be creeping up in countries all over the world. I think that's a direct result of climate change. As all things are inevitably interconnected, what we do to the environment ends up having negative effects to people and nations in far off places around the world.

Climate change ends up affecting politics in the end, as people begin to be concerned about their national economies. This often seems to beckon rogue politicians to be *vomited up* (to use famous author Chris Hedges's words) who craft political ad campaigns that exploit the fear and pandemonium being generated by their political base(s). The body politic any country is capable of voting for fascist dictators and authoritarians who swear that they'll "take care" of all the economic difficulties being caused by natural disasters and the migratory displacement of human beings. What happens when they get elected or install themselves into power is dubious at best and sinister in the worst case scenario.

This book will be about the ill effects of capitalism, money and how a world *without money* could be created should citizens within society ever decided to make the bold decisions that might ultimately do away with the obsolete monetary-reward-value system.

- *If you have ever secretly wondered why humans have to fork over bits of paper and digital digits through financial transaction hallucinations using online banking in "the free market", this book is for you.*
- *If you've ever wondered why there are homeless people*

*living in abject filth on the streets,* then this book is for you.

- *If you instinctively know there is a better way to live and get by in the world,* then this book is *definitely* for you. Maybe you've heard the saying, "Ain't nothin' free in capitalism!" I often think, "Ain't that the truth!"

So without further ado, I'll get down to showing readers what they can do to make the world a much more tranquil place.

# Chapter 1: Capitalism Never Made Any Cents (Sense).

In every basic economics course, students learn about what is claimed to be a free, (but certainly is *not* free) market. *There are always strings attached.* In capitalism, it's always been said that using money is an individual's right to freedom and independence as a form of exchange. Philosophical concepts such as *Value* is placed on particular goods manufactured by seemingly invisible corporations all around the world and profits are made for these mega corporations. Economics professors talk of things like supply and demand issues and gross domestic product GDP. Distribution and manufacturing matters are also discussed in basic economics classes telling the story of how global business enterprises operate. That, as most people understand, is the basic high school and undergraduate college level of understanding of what economics is supposed to be about. Economists love to tout the very dubious notion that free markets are (to use metaphors) "like" a biological ecosystem in which so-called consumers can make free and independent choices about what items and services they wish to purchase.

However, *capitalism and Milton Friedman economics does not tell the whole story.* I don't want to get into the nitty gritty details of comparing the philosophers of economics. I'd rather speak directly to my fellow Americans. In America and other Western nations, money is not just used as a form of exchange, but it has become the very thing itself to possess and so-call "own" (as if anyone or people actually owns anything at all). Ownership of what? People as slaves? People's labor, their time and physical energy? Oh, yes. That's what capitalism demands.

Everyone thinks they're working and being productive producing this service, manufacturing and distributing those goods over there and these necessities over here. In doing this, capitalism uses people's *very selfish human drives, instincts and vices to exploit other human beings.* This ends up causing humanitarian crises, human rights violations and wars all over the world. Anyone ever heard of the global drug trade? American president Richard Nixon's war on drugs has been a complete failure. I'm not here to write about the war on drugs either. That's something other very respectable authors have written about and which I may write about some time in the future. The basic point here is that the concept of poverty is nothing new to anyone who understands and studies economic systems in civilizations past and present.

That brings me to mention that money, assets in the form of property (land, homes, buildings, corporation equipment) becomes a thing to hoard and keep for only a select few people who operate as shareholders and CEO's of mega global conglomerate corporations. Money divides people in terms of vocabulary. Everyone has heard terms like the *working class* (middle class), *the poor, homeless people, wealthy people*, and the *ultra-wealthy*. So that means by using money as the form of exchange means that people live in class systems and class based societies. It's been well researched by author's such as Cornel West in his book *The Rich and The Rest of Us: A Poverty Manifesto* where he writes that *"once a person is born into poverty, they're likely to die poor."* I agree with Dr. West's declaration. This is simply a fact of life for billions of people.

Author Matthew Holten contends that the time has come for money to become a thing of the past in his fascinating and very inspiring book *Moneyless Society – The Next Economic Evolution.* Holten essentially writes that no one hears to much about occupations such as milk men, elevator operators and other obsolete services of the past used primarily in the early 20th century. The notion that most everyone gets into modern elevators to press buttons to get to whatever floor they need in skyscrapers is something everyone takes for granted and doesn't have to think about.

The only way money can become obsolete is for societies is to begin to take steps to make that happen. There's already a movement of people with like minds who envision a world without the use of cash and credit / debit (*debt*) cards. Making monetary transactions to get what one needs to use for a limited time of years, months, weeks, days or hours will simply be a thing of the past. We already live in the era of mass abundance. The Covid-19 pandemic taught us that *work and the supply chain distribution of goods and services can come to a halt in mere hours and days.* This caused a worldwide shortage of everyday necessities. Consequently, people are aware of the fragile nature of "the market place" and the ebbs and flows of economic business.

On a very personal level, I remember as a poor child who had to be taken care of at times in day care centers. The profoundly lonely experience of not being able to go on a few field trips because my parents did not pay (could not afford to pay) was quite traumatizing to me as youngster wondering why so many of the other children were leaving the day care facility. I remember feeling like I was being left behind while most of the other children got to go have fun and do something exciting. That sadness taught me at a very early age that the world was *very unfair. It's unfair because predatory capitalism and the concept of money has been chosen by very rich and powerful people to be the "only way to do business."* The rich and powerful business tycoons,

13

dictators and other politicians of the world have simply decided that money, trading, profits and hoarding wealth is the most important thing in human existence.

In preparing to write this book I've had to do a decent amount of studying and research to understand what other authors, academics and intellectuals are currently saying about poverty, money, capitalism and fascism. Side Note: A funny irony here is I've read two books written by two authors with the first name Matthew. Matthew Desmond writes in *Poverty, By America* that about two-thirds of all student college tuition debt is "held by African American females". So that brings not only *class*, but *race* into this equation.

Why does it make economic sense *(cents)* to wage war by invading other countries just to steal *allegedly valuable* land and natural resources? Why does it make sense to murder innocent human beings in the form of "collateral damage" during wars of capitalism that go on for decades at a time? Again, it is because super rich oligarchs, dictators, powerful politicians and their sycophants believe that conducting the business of war is inevitable and necessary in order to keep the status quo (capitalism & money) circulating in the forms of transactions between humans in every country on planet Earth. The idea that no public intellectual anywhere seems to critique such nefarious operations enough is beyond me.

Another way money and capitalist commerce dealings

doesn't make sense is that of all the animals in that animal kingdom, we humans are the "only mammals to wear pants", to borrow a phrase from alternative rock band Pearl Jam's 2001 hit song *Do the Evolution.* Performing financial transactions in the form of spending bits of paper and electronic hallucinations is something unique to the human species. Such hallucinations are done in mere seconds on the Internet and in various stores and other places known as businesses. There are mom and pop (small) businesses and the freakish mega global conglomerate venture capital entities known as mega-corporations.

Scientists don't observe birds participating in such behavior. No other animal does this. The whole idea of survival of the fittest is really a misunderstood concept. While tigers and crocodiles must behave predatorily in order to continue living, social animals such as primates don't necessarily always have to behave predatorily. Sure, chimpanzees will behave pathologically in the form of rape and capture, but other primates are more cooperative and act in the form of doing what's best for the entire group.

It seems that it's only we humans who're truly the "cruel animals" of the animal kingdom. It seems that part of our cruelty has been in the form of creating systems of barbarism, feudalism, serfdom, slavery, capitalism and fascism. Anyone who really takes a step back and observes human behavior understands that a large percentage of the human population has simply become victims of a rather

15

small number of fellow humans who insist on behaving in predatory manners. Such behavior has caused what scientists have been trying to warn us about for many decades now. Climate change should have been dealt with many yesterdays' ago, but somehow is still not being properly dealt with. What's happening as I write this is that climate change is being thought by some people to be fueling a historical pendulum shift in many countries from democracy into fascism. That kind of does make sense though.

When you think of all the dollars and cents we've been crazily concerned with and hoarding for thousands of years, it seems at times that money will never ever go away. *It may not ever go away.* That is something that we must think about and possibly accept even if many of us don't wish to.

Even so, those of us who envision the idea that there *can* be another way of conducting human business affairs, understand that a new economy will have to eventually be created. An economy that creates a system that uses our abundant resources in a way that provides for the basic needs of most (if not every) human being on planet Earth will simply be an eventual and very transitional process and experience. I know that sounds like a pipe dream – a perfect world scenario, but I personally believe it can be achieved. Others do too. Humans have been cooperating together more than being extremely selfish for most of our existence. Capitalism may force us to currently live and behave in extremely selfish and insane ways, but that doesn't mean it

16

should or will always be that way. That is, if we choose to exist in a better way. *If we choose to just keep going down this very Earth destructing path, then* we won't be able to experience what very well *"could" be achieved* if only we *get our collective heads out of the proverbial sand and begin to address global climate change in a truly responsible way.* The choice I think needs to me made is that we don't need to make money at all. What we must do *is to simply make money become obsolete!*

*If we do not take the opportunities* that we still have to make such a needed change, then we'll continue to have our homes flooded, people will become displaced and have to migrate to other nations that might accept them as refugees which only increases and continues the humanitarian crises humans are experiencing right this very moment. Just last night I watched national news discussing extreme weather events that are essentially unprecedented and haven't occurred in about 100 years. Many climate scientists and activists are telling us right now that we humans are in what's being called the "age of extinction." Take note of that. What does that really mean? I don't think it means take another sip of coffee and continue watching television. What means is leaders and policy makers in countries all over the world must take notice and begin to make the changes that might mitigate the devastating effects of global climate change.

It's obvious I'm not the only author exploiting the

opportunity to write about climate change to sell books and "make money" in the current economic system of capitalism. Money has been psychologically reinforced as an emotional and physical need through operant conditioning and Pavlovian behaviorism. Money has been reinforced by being a "reward-value system" in operation. Our very innate human instincts force us to want something as a "reward" for good behavior, hard work and producing physical items and performing vital services needed in society. It's only natural to want such things. However, it must be also reinforced that selfish and cruel human behavior is not okay. If humans can achieve the same ends using different means – means of cooperation rather than predatory competition, then true progress can be made. Progress is something progressive liberals such as myself really do believe in. The idea of being free from something is not a pipe dream. Just as people can behave in self-preserving ways, humans can act in ways that enhance the survival of other humans and animals in the animal kingdom.

Other ways in which capitalism doesn't make any sense is in people's attitudes and perceptions of people who're poor, unemployed or do things for which no money is never made. The idea that one's quote "success" depends on how much money he or she makes is exceedingly popular here in America and many other countries. The American (mostly Christian) Puritan work ethic is reinforced into many people's minds as way of being in the world. People talk about the virtues of hard work and financial success. I don't have to elaborate too much to paint the picture many are already familiar with of television pundits and figure heads touting the obsession of getting rich quick, financial workshops, personal finance budgeting gimmicks and books claiming to turn ordinary people into financial tycoons and captains of industry. The talk of being an entrepreneur is a very coveted title in America. The popular cliché if you don't work, you don't eat is said over and over again to reinforce the idea that if one is not making money, their activities and existence doesn't make any sense.

Finally, to wrap up this chapter, I'll discuss something that has always been very funny to me. Humor is often the best antidote to many of our anxieties. One of my all-time favorite rock bands They Might Be Giants, of Brooklyn, New York recorded a track for a 1991 B-sides compilation album titled *Miscellaneous-T*. The track is simply titled "13" and is an audio recording of a New York City resident named Gloria who's having a difficult time discussing the concept of a service for which no money is made. The lyrical dialogue of a three-way phone conversation is listed on the next page for your enjoyment:

19

**THEY MIGHT BE GIANTS' *MISCELLANEOUS-T*,**

**TRACK "13." © 1991**

"**Gloria:** What do you think--what do you make out of that recording?

**Guy on Phone:** I don't know, Gloria, I just don't--

**Gloria:** Some kind of singing. They sound like all kinds of people, right?

**Guy on Phone:** Yeah.

**Gloria:** And then it says, "Another child is born in India every time you call this number," right?

**Guy on Phone:** Yeah, right.

**Gloria:** Does that make any sense to you?

**Guy on Phone:** No, it doesn't make no sense to me.

**Gloria:** Bu--and the guy that spoke--I don't know who he is.

**Guy on Phone:** Yeah.

**Gloria:** But that--that--it doesn't sound like no answering machine, right?

**Guy on Phone:** No, it ain't an answering machine

20

because they're not saying anything; they just--

**Gloria:** But what does he get--*how does he make money on this?* Whatever he's advertising in the paper. *This is the part that don't make no sense.*

**Guy on Phone:** Oh, he's advertising this in the paper you saw it.

**Gloria:** In the Village Voice, yeah. They got--that's where the Kiss Clinic, but they give you another number if you wanna join it. Then I got the "intellectuals meet with other intellectuals..."

**Guy on Phone:** Yeah.

**Gloria:** ...speak another language.

**Guy on Phone:** Yeah. Oh.

**Gloria:** They meet at La Met--La Maisonette restaurant. They give you the price. Then they give you another number to call if you're interested. This guy... all you get is this here recording, but u-w--*I don't see how he makes money.*

**Guy on Phone:** Yeah, yeah.

**Gloria:** You know what I'm saying? It's just.... They got the craziest things in that paper.

**Guy on Phone:** Yeah, yeah.

**Gloria:** They come over with all--they got the craziest

21

things. But this one here-- "There Must Be Giants," it's called. And it says "call machine," and they got the phone number.

**Guy on Phone:** Yeah.

**Gloria:** But what kind of money does he make? It don't make no sense. Well, he don't make any money, right?

**Guy on Phone:** No.

**Gloria:** But, that's--then he's a nut, right? Do you see-do you see any sense to that? "There May Be Giants?" That reco--that recording I have on. The new one. Did you hear it? I changed it. I took off the intellectuals. I put on There May Be Giants.

**Guy in Background:** What?

**Gloria:** Who's They May Be Giants?

**Guy in Background:** What are you talking about?

**Gloria:** That's what's on my--the phone, There May Be

G-- well I can't explain it, 'cause I don't know what it is.

**Guy in Background:** (unintelligible muttering) you could make sense once in a while.

**Gloria:** Look in the paper! Don't blame me if the guy's a nut."

**Footnote:** The above dialogue was taken from "This Might Be a Wiki – The TMBG Knowledge Base" website: *https://tmbw.net/wiki/Lyrics:Untitled*

# Chapter 2: Capitalism Has Anti-Social Personality Disorder

In chapter one, I discussed how capitalism and using money to exploit people not only doesn't make a lot of sense, but that it is often referred to using words such as predatory to describe its ill effects. In this chapter, I wish to articulate the concept that money is essentially an antisocial contract that strangles and suffocates not only the poor, but the very rich as well. I'll attempt to argue that by having a system put into place that separates people by class and race, money simply exacerbates such separation by causing so many unnecessary conditions and problems for everyone involved in living in America and other countries.

When I say money is antisocial, I am referring to the concept known in psychology as APD or *antisocial-personality disorder*. I remember viewing a documentary titled *The Corporation,* a 2003 Canadian documentary film

24

written by University of British Columbia law professor Joel Bakan and filmmaker Harold Crooks. The documentary examines the modern corporation. Bakan wrote a book titled *The Corporation: The Pathological Pursuit of Profit and Power*. As I watched the film, I was quite taken back and astonished to learn that if the modern corporation were to be examined as a person, corporations would be diagnosed with antisocial-personality disorder. As a student of psychology myself with only two years of community college, I'll list the *DSM-V's* official criteria psychologists use to determine if a person has APD below:

Symptoms & criteria for antisocial personality disorder

According to the *DSM-5*, there are four diagnostic criteria, of which Criterion A has seven sub-features.

**Disregard for and violation of others rights since age 15, as indicated by one of the seven sub features:**

Failure to obey laws and norms by engaging in behavior which results in criminal arrest, or would warrant criminal arrest

Lying, deception, and manipulation, for profit or self-amusement,

Impulsive behavior

Irritability and aggression, manifested as frequently assaults others, or engages in fighting

Blatantly disregards safety of self and others,

A pattern of irresponsibility and

Lack of remorse for actions *(American Psychiatric Association, 2013)*

The other diagnostic Criterion are:

**The person is at least age 18**

**Conduct disorder was present before age 15**

**The antisocial behavior does not occur in the context of schizophrenia or bipolar disorder *(American Psychiatric Association, 2013)***

As many readers probably already know, society uses the term psychopath to refer to bad actors as being evil, villainous, murderous and are often depicted as craven serial killers and rapists. Though this is often the case in actual crimes committed by perpetrators who end up eventually getting arrested and put in jail or prison, many people may not be aware of or understand that modern corporations do act like villainous psychopaths as well alongside single individual people. If corporations were depicted in films and television dramas on Netflix or BritBox as being craven serial murderers, people would be much more reluctant to do business with many of the well-known corporate entities such as Amazon and Apple. Corporations exploit workers everyday all over the world. Workers are forced to work long hours in abject conditions and circumstances. It's been well-documented that Amazon's warehouses are many workers' worst nightmare. Workers are timed as to how often and how quick they use the restroom. Some have reported urinating in water bottles in order to not have to make a trip to the often very far away and often in-use restrooms that are available.

Social scientists and other researchers are well aware of the Apple – Fox Con controversy where Chinese workers have been worked into utter exhaustion. What benevolent corporate entity would allow their workers to live in such abysmal conditions? It seems more likely that predatory and psychopathic organizations and institutions require workers and staff to undergo immense psychological pain, confusion and exhaustion in order to create products and services the modern world demands in the 21$^{st}$ Century. What kind of employer would exploit workers by forcing them to urinate into water bottles?

Workers who feel they have to do that are in a very real way individuals who're being held hostage by the fact that they have not only their own mouths to feed, but the mouths of their children and other family members. People don't work in such horrid conditions because they want to, they do so because often they have to. Corporations know this.

That's why they often do get away with creating work environments that cause such misery. Workers have to work themselves like zombies because we humans live in a world where money is the only thing that matters. Profits over people is a common saying one hears in discussions about politics, capitalism and the problems caused by vast inequality and poverty in America (one of the richest nations in the world).

True crime television or book buffs are well aware of the concept of kidnapping individuals in order to receive some sort of ransom payments or to cause problems for law enforcement officers tasked with tracking down missing persons and victims of violence. Corporations essentially kidnap workers by forcing them to work in unsafe conditions and do unsafe things in order to maximize profits to make corporate shareholders and CEO's amass an inordinate amount of personal wealth while the workers that make them filthy rich only get by paycheck to paycheck. If you've ever heard or read that most Americans are about two paychecks away from personal financial catastrophe, then you understand that corporate shareholders and CEO's are the ones responsible for such antisocial behavior and conditions that exist within the workplace.

Right now at this very moment, I am an average poor U.S. citizen living in the city of San Diego, California. San Diego is one of the wealthiest cities in America. Ever since I got out of the U.S. Marine Corps, I have been mentally and in many cases physically disabled. I've tried applying for SSI disability three times with negative results. I've only completed two years of college. I dropped out before student loan debt became too high. That was in 2005. My four year honorable Marine Corp career began in June of 1998 and ended in June of 2002. I now I'm fortunate enough to not have had to go serve in Iraq or Afghanistan. To all U.S. veterans who may read this, please know that I salute all who've given their lives and who were severely traumatized and wounded in those capitalistic forever-wars.

Since leaving the military, I've worked as a freelance web and graphic designer. My 2023 hobby of trying to get my foot into the author business is quite challenging. At any rate, I'm doing what I can and just taking one day at a time like everyone else.

News pundits tell us not to panic. Pundits writing articles and discussing AI in the media tell us that there will still be jobs available for humans to do (for example graphic design or accounting). Oh, okay. *Good.* But those same humans will now be *competing against – AI.* Oh, and guess what? *Pay will be much lower.* Salaries will be slashed and workers will be scrambling for whatever jobs continue to exist until AI & capitalism has exhausted industries and individual human beings to the point of no decay and collapse.

To wrap this chapter up, I shall remark on the very nature of capitalism. It is one of *exploitation and manipulation.* First, man manipulates the natural environment in the process of acquiring all the natural resources that are to be used in the production and maintenance of "product X" or "service X." Capitalism ends up extracting as many resources available until existential exhaustion. Then they switch over to other parts of the world to cleave out and mine other natural resources such as nickel for electric cars like Tesla batteries in countries around the world. It seems that nothing is off limits to global capitalism. *There's no land on planet Earth that capitalism is not willing to exploit and destroy.*

This exploitation until destruction doesn't just take place within physical entities and objects such as oil, plastic and wood, but *people* end up being used and manipulated in the process as well. People's labor is the first thing used up in capitalist dealings. People end up manipulating each other while offering their own labor in the work place in exchange for whatever they can get because they know that in the work place, everyone is being exploited and used for something. Something "has to always be 'in it' for them." Thus, people have no problems using and abusing each other. Bullying in the workplace is something I've experienced time and time again for being perceived as gay during my service during Don't Ask, Don't Tell (DADT) that excluded gays and lesbians from serving openly and honestly in the U.S military. This process of exploitation and manipulation is the hallmark of predatory behavior.

Exploitation and manipulation is the hallmark of predatory psychopaths and people who have been diagnosed with anti-social-personality disorder. Whether we call them psychopaths or sociopaths, the key ingredient here is that their behavior is exploitative and manipulative. Capitalism as our economic system and money as a means of getting our most daily needs met is the proverbial fuel for predators' deceitful behavior. There's no secret to this. Mainstream media and even Internet media entities simply ignore capitalism as a culprit to humanities woes.

When you compare many corporations' overall behavior to that of actual individual people - that's when you can begin to make the connection between what "society does" and what we as individuals do. Psychologists seem to have discovered a link between societal antisocial behavior and individual CEO's who run huge corporations. There are books written about billionaire oligarchs such as Elon Musk and Jeff Bezos. Psychologists argue that if "corporations are people" – well, then – corporations are behaving in ways psychopaths and sociopaths behave. We have sociologists who study such things as corporations. Sociologists work with psychologists to study individual human beings' behaviors. It seems they've concluded the notion that corporations and the people that run them are essentially behaving antisocially.

Destroy Capitalism Before It Destroys Us! | Shawn Gillick

# Chapter 3: Many Social, Political, Natural & Economic Problems Can Be Traced Back to Capitalism

For decades, I have had a sense that "something is not right" about the way we humans live our lives. As far back as when I served in the United States Marine Corps, I noticed that it felt like I was living in a "rat race." I would even hear other co-workers (marines) comment about "the rat race." We would sort of laugh it all off sort of tongue-in-cheek. "That's just part of life, I guess." We'd say. But whenever I was in my "off time" on the weekends, I would always have this nagging thought in the back of my mind that something about "shopping" and "going to the mall" was kind of a bad way to spend one's free time. The nagging feeling was more like: "*there has got to be more to life than this*." Shopping, spending money and going from one strip mall to another was not a thrilling or fulfilling way of living (for me). I was 24 when I first began feeling almost nauseous and certainly "weird" about shopping and related dealings. It turns out, that was only the beginning. Those nagging feelings and thoughts about shopping often lead me to conduct my own "research" into related phenomena. I would read books published by sociologists and cultural critics such as *Naomi Klein*. I read Naomi Klein's *The Shock Doctrine – The Rise of Disaster Capitalism,* published in 2007. Her book was the

33

first "anti-capitalist" book I ever read. From that point on, I had a fire burning in my belly. I had to learn as much about capitalism as I could in order to be a good opinion leader. In order to help make the world a better place, it was incumbent upon me to know as much about capitalism aside from majoring in or taking actual economics courses (LOL!).

When I pay attention to the news, I often see headlines (in American news) alerting readers that there's been another mass shooting. Like clock-work, the headlines are generated, published and aggregated across the entire Internet. I'd surmise that by now, even people living under rocks have heard about the uniquely American cultural phenomenon known as "*mass shootings*". Workplace shootings, shootings that occur in and around shopping malls or in big-box-stores like Walmart, school shootings, church shootings, synagogue shootings and anywhere outside in a public place shootings occur with frighteningly increasing frequency. They occur so often that most of us are at some point psychologically numb to it all.

We care, yes – we do care about the poor victims of mass shootings, but we have to be able to put our heads down on our pillows at night and be able to sleep without worrying too much about the victims and their families of such violence. Each time a mass shooting occurs, we sigh huge sighs of relief knowing that we and people we know and love were not shot dead within the blink of an eye. We "knock on wood" in feeling grateful that we haven't been slaughtered yet. What bothers me about all this is that journalists always ask "why?" Or "Who would do such a thing?" Like it's some kind of mystery. Very often we hear the question "What was the shooter's motive?" Journalists will be sure to ask "was the mass shooting racially motivated?" They'll ask, "Was it a hate crime?" Journalists and investigators will look at the minute details of each crime (which is always important), but many of them will fail to take a step back and ask questions about the general way the victims and perpetrators of mass shootings were living their lives.

One question I never hear journalists ask is "Could capitalism be a motive in any of these kinds of crimes?" *Could it be that the people who commit such heinous acts have been put "through proverbial hell" by life?*

Does anyone ever ask questions about capitalism like "is it humane to have to constantly be on one's toes, having to constantly be sure that one doesn't miss a day's work because the rent is due at the first of the month. One has to pay for *everything* in his or her life. This constant *having-to-pay-for-everything* takes an almost inevitable toll on people. *Could it be that people just up and "snap" because of all pressure (both social and financial) they've been put through in life?*

The pressure to succeed. The pressure to make good grades. The pressure to not get pulled over by the police. The pressure of having to pay so many fines and fees (*i.e.,* court fees for parking tickets). In every situation where a person has to make a financial transaction, *there is a certain amount of emotional and psychological pressure put onto people.* The pressure builds up. It exists, because people know they have to keep enough money in their checking or savings accounts to pay DMV fees, court fees, library late book fees and all the other fees & bills accrued on a daily-monthly-annul basis. Such pressure to succeed and have all of one's financial dealings in perfect order can cause (in my opinion) someone to essentially say "fuck it" and do something terrible.

First let me be clear in saying that I in no way condone any kind of mass shooting or shooting spree (or any act of violence). At no time is it ever appropriate to commit murder just because one's life is in disarray. However, one has to posit that it is at least prudent of us to ask the question: *"Can capitalism cause mass murder?"*

In answering that very question, I can already say that "yes" capitalism can and does cause mass murder indirectly in that the system of capitalism has allowed people so set up a marketplace where any psychologically deranged individual can make legal purchases of assault rifles without a background check or waiting period. Infamous "ghost guns" have become commonplace in American crimes within the last few years. Ghost guns are guns that apparently cannot be traced back to the purchaser or manufacture. The Internet has made it possible (through capitalism) for angry people to order parts & pieces required

36

to build firearms at home. Would be gun makers can then make their own homemade gun parts using 3-D printers and templates sold or distributed for free on the "dark web."

Mass gun violence is just one issue to discuss. One social problem that can directly be associated with capitalism is homelessness. Just today I was walking down the sidewalk in my neighborhood here in San Diego, California when I noticed what looked like an elderly man using a walker passed out on the lawn of a home behind my apartment building. My neighborhood is known for being safe and upscale, but many of the city's homeless population do wander through and this was no exception. What struck me though about this situation was that I thought the individual was perhaps unconscious or worse (dead). I went over to him and tapped his leg gently with my foot and he woke up. He began telling me to call an ambulance or the police so he could "go to jail." I told him that he wouldn't be going to jail...but that I would call for an ambulance if he really needed one. After speaking with him for a few minutes, I discovered no phone call was necessary. He was just another San Diego citizen down on his luck and homeless either through some faults of his own (obviously), but also because of forces that are completely out of his control. As I stood there speaking to him, I felt shameful and pathetic to not really be able to help him like I'd like to be able to. I'd like to cure homelessness, but I know that's not possible. Even the most "socialist" or moneyless society couldn't "cure" homelessness. There would likely be people who would (for some reason or another) be homeless, roaming the streets. However, I believe in my heart that a better world is possible and that's why I'm writing this book. Humans have the potential to make the world a more hospitable place for everyone, including the citizens of the world who're currently and technically homeless or displaced.

In my past, I was close to homelessness and technically kind of still am. Even so, I'm far better off than many people who're just a couple paychecks away from being evicted from their homes. Imagine – *just a couple* paychecks away from utter personal and financial catastrophe! The COVID-19 pandemic really brought this into the national spotlight when it was revealed just how close many American citizens are to being evicted from their homes and apartments. The eviction moratoriums have been lifted and it's "business as usual" for capitalists who hold so much financial power over other human beings. I remember not many people enjoyed the conditions during lockdown. But, it did bring people closer together for those early few weeks and months in a way that no one expected.

People began re-thinking their lifestyles and occupations. People found different priorities – priorities that were not tied to capitalism. If anything, we saw just how fragile capitalism is during the pandemic. Supply chain disruptions and consumers hoarding toilet paper and hand sanitizer made numerous headlines in the early weeks of the pandemic. Unlike a robust "ecosystem" that really allows living beings to thrive, capitalism seems downright fragile. It is fraught with one problem after another. It is certainly not the efficient life-like system so many pro-capitalist economists would like for people to believe. If one looks back at the time many Americans were sheltering in place, mass shootings came to a halt. I don't remember hearing about any during that time and I was glued to the television to keep up on all the COVID-19 news and information. Because I haven't actually checked (even though I probably should), I'm assuming that doesn't mean no mass shootings occurred at all, but what it does mean is that we didn't see any major headlines of mass shootings during the early days of the pandemic because everyone (most everyone) was held up inside either a home, hotel room or shelter of some kind. I would wager that most of the would be mass shooters were mitigating and taking precautions for self-preservations reasons just like everyone else. That doesn't necessarily have a direct correlation or cause – effect relationship to capitalism per se, but it's definitely something to notice.

I'm not in any way insinuating that society should "lock down" again or behave in any way like it did during the pandemic, but I do think we should destroy capitalism before it continues to destroy us from the inside out and the world we live in. That would not in any way solve all or even most of the many social problems humans experience on a daily basis, but it would be a huge and drastic first step. I'm not naïve though. I don't live in a utopia and I don't believe in entertaining too many pipe dreams. But, I do – in my heart of hearts believe that a TRANSITION from our current form of capitalism into *something else* can and *must* be done. I'd like to see money done away with altogether. But again, that will take (in my mind) a definite transitionary period where money (i.e., some good aspects of capitalism) will still be used or needed whenever absolutely necessary. The transition doesn't have to be too long either.

I'm not pretentious enough to even think I could come up with a "timeline" of transitioning over to a moneyless society. However, I can imagine what I think it could entail and discuss other aspects of what might need to happen during a transition phase. I think it would most certainly be "evolutionary" in nature. It took countless years for capitalism to appear in human life, so I am realistic enough to presume that it shall take some amount of time to transition to a better (more equitable) system.

Matthew Holten wrote about "systems" in his book *Moneyless Society*. He writes about what he thinks could or should happen by studying various systems though a more scientific and engineering perspective. Since I hold no special degrees of any kind, I'll leave the minutia of such new systems for authors with more expertise and knowledge. Perhaps they can put things into better perspective for readers interested in precise details about what sorts of systems would need to be crafted for a transition from capitalism over to something better. When I read about

Holten's rather telling example of "the milk man", I became further obsessed with conducting a philosophical investigation into what it could and will take in order to make money become utterly obsolete.

I remember being quite fascinated to be reminded of obsolete occupations that used to actually exist. Who thinks of occupations such as milkmen or elevator operators these days? Only in some rare or extreme exceptions, such occupations are nonexistent. Another problem for me as a philosopher critiquing capitalism is the rather arbitrary notion of "price". For instance, as a self-published author, I have to market my book and set prices for each book *and each format of each book. I have always found pricing and prices to be utterly arbitrary and absurd.* Now I know economists have studied and done all the math necessary to conclude why certain prices should or ought to be set for certain products and services.

Corporations hire people with backgrounds in math and economics to crunch all the numbers and they rely on various rules and standards that have been set forth in all industries where products and services are sold and distributed. On some level, it all makes some kind of sense. But on another (more existential) level, I find absurdity in just about everything to do with commerce dealings and capitalism. Perhaps the existentialist in me has influenced my bias against marketplace shenanigans and capitalist theater. People who sell products online are often amazed at how one

41

price point yields more sales than others for the same exact product! There's definitely some psychology and mathematics taking place when determining how much something should cost. But, I personally find that to be a problem because of things like price gouging, inflation and *"shrinkflation."* Entire books can be written about the process of our food shrinking, sizes of packaging constantly changing shape. Are my Cheetos actually getting smaller or is it just me? Something's been happening to our food.

In the next chapter, I will discuss the problem of human greed and money through the lens of philosophy and psychology.

# Chapter 4: Selfishness and greed is the fuel of capitalism

Before we get started here – let me say a few words about something that irritates the heck out of me: government shutdowns. As I'm writing this, American news headlines are instilling propaganda-like fear into the hearts and minds of unassuming readers about the government shutting down. It seems like whenever a liberal president or liberal administration holds power in the Oval Office, republicans scream bloody murder about things like the national financial deficit and threaten to shut down the entire economy by shutting down the federal government. These threats sometimes do come into fruition and become reality for many millions of Americans. However – notice that these loud-mouthed republican politicians get paid during government shutdowns. Shutting government down rarely (if ever) has any direct consequence or result in their personal lives. That's not true for the millions of people whose lives are directly affected by government shutting down even for a small amount of time. Such a topic brings me to discuss the very human behaviors of selfishness and greed.

Many of us have the ability to regulate at least *some* of our major selfish desires and tendencies towards being greedy. However, our economic system has no moral compass to use as a means of regulating such behavior. Since the Supreme Court (what I currently call the "subpar court") decided that "corporations are people" – I've concluded that capitalism behaves like a cravenly selfish and greedy psychopath. Psychopaths have malignant narcissism built into their pathology and abnormal personality structure. (see chapter 2). I must also note that every human being (according to most psychologists) have innate traits and behavioral characteristics that cause us to behave in ways associated with all the known personality disorders studied by social scientists. Even so, just because we innate biological and environmental tendencies that allow us to act selfishly and greedily, that certainly does not mean it's in society's best interest for each individual to cravenly behave that way with reckless disregard for others. Manners and being polite goes a long way. Having a code of ethics and social customs (etiquette) has taken our species a very long way in terms of biological evolution. Cooperating with one another and behaving in socially accepted and "appropriate" ways is essential for groups of people as large as "entire civilizations" to co-exist in relative peace and harmony.

That brings me to discuss the concept we have all heard of known as *intrinsic rewards versus extrinsic rewards*. Capitalism, is by default, a system *built to exploit* our need for extrinsic rewards. Money is the epitome of extrinsic rewarding. I often use the term *"monetary-reward-value-system"* when referring to money and working for it. There are many examples I could list and ramble on about that illustrate both forms of psychological rewards. I want to dive into the nitty-gritty here and discuss ways that one might still be able to work and thrive in a society that didn't use money as its primary form of extrinsic reward. As a thought-experiment, let us presume that we're now living in a world where money is completely obsolete. What would you (we) do? What you do with your time and skills? You've gone to college or worked in an occupation for many years gaining skills and knowledge to create things and do a varying manner of things. *Just what would you do? Why would you do it?*

With no monetary bits of paper in the form of cash or numerical digits in various bank accounts for you to draw upon (credit / debit cards), how would you go about obtaining goods and necessities needed to survive? How would this new society manufacture and distribute things (products and services) in *an equitable manner* so that *all people within the society get their most basic universal needs met?* My big presumption here is that many (if not most) people would continue creating and doing things that not only benefit themselves, but benefit others as well. *We would still find meaning in our lives.* We'd still find purpose in what we made or gathered throughout the day. We would still exchange things and share things with each other. We'd create jobs that allow for the easy distribution of daily necessities. I'm sure many people would even still hoard things they thought were useful. People would still make and want their "nick-knacks-and-paddy-whacks!"

Despite the fact that history has shown what humans are capable of when adapting to change and overcoming obstacles. The occupational and very physical practice of engineering is what humans are really good at. So *why not engineer a new way – a new system of living and doing things using the same systems and engineering solutions we in place right this minute?* We can "be-and-exist-in-the-world" without money! What exactly is holding us back? I think our selfishness and greedy tendencies are preventing us from moving forward with creating a new system.

Until we learn that we don't have to have "that monetary-reward" at the end of each project or at the end of each day, we'll continue to think we "have to always have something in it for us." The "What's-in-it-for-me?" mentality has caused many of the problems we currently face. Corporations always behave in the "What's-in-it-for-me?" mindset. Now I understand completely that the jobs and actual things people create and do on a day-to-day basis would (and will) drastically change in a new (moneyless) system. What one does with his or her time would likely be drastically different. But, people would *still* be doing something…lest they really do wish to just "sit around all day doing absolutely nothing." Maybe. Some people would obviously be doing that. Many are already doing that. That's nothing new.

I guess – my hunch is that most-everyone will get tired of just sitting around and they'll begin to find productive ways to spend their time. And by productive, I mean that literally – producing goods (nick-knacks-and-paddy-whacks) for all to enjoy and consume. How a new society would be "governed" and how rules and regulations would be enforced can all be decided and will have to be decided. That's all up for discussion and thinking about NOW because we don't have much more time to be wasting. What we've done through capitalism to the environment has caused and quickly causing monumental changes in the way we humans must live our lives. Capitalism-induced extreme weather and natural disaster events are killing and displacing humans in the possible "era of mass human extinction" right this second!

To wrap up this chapter, I will make sure to mention the fact that I know it's difficult for many people (myself included) to overcome some of our more impulsive, selfish and greedy tendencies. I also know that there are some people who will never be able to gain enough insight into their own behavior in order make necessary changes in how they live their lives. Those people will continue to be selfish and greedy even in a money-free society. The rest of us (which I think is most people) will be able to adapt their behavior enough so that they can alter their lifestyles according to the new unspoken rules of the new society. The new system could be a hybrid of capitalism and socialism. It could be socialism in a form we've never experimented with or had before. It could be a completely money-less society and system. Whatever it is, it has to be a more humane system. Because right now – capitalism is profoundly inhumane. Just the other night, I watched a documentary detailing with the trials and tribulations of the American (& global) workplace.

The COVID-19 pandemic altered our very way of working both in the office and with our hands doing things outside and at home. People's homes became the new office space. Even before the pandemic, the future of work was dubious and being discussed. There are forces such as automation (robotics, driverless vehicles, etc.) and there's *"Artificial Intelligence (AI)" which has upended entire occupations.* As I may have alluded to earlier in my book, AI is already a force to be reckoned with. We evidently cannot escape the next technological revolution. It's already here and many people are wondering where they fit into the work world. As a freelance graphic artist and former web designer, I saw the writing on the wall years ago and stopped being a web designer and simply continued honing my craft of graphic design – but now AI has upended industries such as graphic design and other occupations that deal with computing technology (such as accounting, etc.).

In the *PBS documentary (I think it was titled The Future of Work),* they mentioned one force that is driving much of the current changes in the workforce: "profit" – and what is profit, but one of the main themes of capitalism. Corporations are making exceptionally high profits during this era of the 21st century. What is driving the profits? *I and many others think it is human greed!* The CEOs, shareholders and other captains of industry are hoarding massive amounts of wealth and assets all because their human greed has collectively driven the price of literally everything to skyrocket. Also, corporations have always sought ways to make more profits with fewer and fewer workers. Corporations will use fewer employees and resources for those employees. They'll use artificial intelligence wherever and however they can if it means cutting healthcare costs and other perks for the employees they hire. That means that whomever is left working for a given company is competing not only against other humans in need of the same job...but they're effectively competing against artificial intelligence, algorithms and automation as well! All their hard work is being done and will continue to be done with less pay, thus forcing said workers to have to work two and three jobs in "the gig economy" just to survive.

How is any of this humane? It's not. It never was. Everyone by now has heard of child labor – especially in other (third world) countries. It's trying to make a comeback here in America. I'm not here to talk about that right now. What I will say on that topic is that it's quite anti-society (antisocial) to force children to work and drop out of school so they can work to help their parents survive because changes of the capitalist economy have occurred. Really? People don't know how lucky they are to be able to send their children to school here in America. As bad as our current public education system is, things could be much worse. The idea that any child in any country should have to quit school and go to work is abominable. It's repugnant. Not only is capitalism rapacious, it's also quite repugnant. I don't even have children. My husband and I have chosen not to ever adopt children. (BTW: I'm not really married. I simply live with my gay domestic partner). I cannot fathom bringing a child into this world for any reason. I know many women seem to have a biological, spiritual and philosophical calling to have children…but I wish they would think twice before getting pregnant and having "those adorable babies." The world we're living is in veritable shambles – and that's not doom's day talk. These are facts. I mean – the sky isn't necessarily falling down (the last time I checked it wasn't). But our Earth sure is being scorched by the Sun and climate change. Global warming, the CO2 problem and ice glaciers melting are all real problems that we have to deal with. Wildfires, destructive hurricanes and other natural disasters are displacing humans in many nations as I type this. Are you really proud of yourself for getting pregnant? I hope you are able to sustain and maintain your quality of life during your pregnancy and afterwards. Capitalism isn't going to make your life any easier. Of course I'm directing these words at pregnant women readers. The rest of us shall want to make women's lives a bit more comfortable by doing what we can to destroy capitalism and get rid of the problems effecting and affecting women's health. Abortion should be made legal ALL ACROSS the land (not only in America, but everywhere!). That's a topic for another book…but I mention it here because it does tie in with the topic of this chapter and the entire theme of the book. Selfish and greedy humans are making life difficult for others to live their lives. Much of this is being done through existential changes and choices via capitalism, but religion and politics also has a huge part to play. But again, those other issues could be discussed in another book. Successfully destroying capitalism is more difficult than it seems on the surface. A transitionary period will have to be implemented. I hope it can happen sooner rather than in decades and hundreds of years. Right now, no one knows if such a thing can possibly even happen. I'm sure most reading this probably think the dream of destroying capitalism is merely a pipe dream or utopia-like thinking.

My previous book was entitled *New Existentialism – A New Philosophy for the 21ˢᵗ Century*. I wrote a lot about religion, politics and of course the philosophy of existentialism. In existentialism, there are themes. One major theme is that of *human freedom*. The famous existentialist philosopher Jean-Paul Sartre once wrote *we are "condemned to be free."* Well, I suppose so. But then again – living in a capitalist world, *we have condemned ourselves to become work drones and slaves for the economic system of capitalism. If we are so condemned to be free – why aren't we insisting that we live free lives?* I mean – *truly* free lives? As it stands right now – we're not. Nothing is free in "free-market capitalism." In the next chapter, I will write about how capitalism is very much "like" a cult. I somehow seem to be stopping short of calling it an actual cult…because at least people can escape cults. As of right now – I'm not convinced people can (truly) and safely escape the grasp of capitalism. Stay tuned…. Or just turn / move onto the next page!

# Chapter 5: Capitalism as a Cult

As a lifelong student of psychology and philosophy, I have studied (and wrote an unpublished manuscript about) cults and cult-like organizations. Interestingly enough, I've been able to see many cult-like qualities that exist within capitalism that many people have probably never noticed or discussed before. I will attempt to list as many off the top of my head here with a brief analysis of capitalism through the lens of an armchair social psychologist and philosopher. Notice that I'm stopping well short of proclaiming that capitalism *is* a cult. I'm not currently qualified to make such a declaration. Despite what I personally might think or "like" to say – that's just something I'll leave for more qualified experts to proclaim.

On second thought, perhaps I am qualified enough. After all, I am…a consumer in capitalism. I'm a U.S. citizen who spends cash in various vending buildings known as brick and mortar stores. I've been traumatized by not being able to afford certain necessities throughout my life. So maybe I am perfectly qualified to discuss capitalism through the lens of social scientists who hypothesize that capitalism has many cult-like qualities. I'm a victim of capitalism. As such, I shall pen down whatever words I wish in order to craft a scathing analysis of capitalists and the economic system love so much. We could even conclude that capitalism has gurus and cult-like figures at the top who run the *cult of capitalism*. Men like Milton Friedman and others who promote the (*not*) free market, and all its plastic claptrap. We can indeed proclaim that the gurus of capitalism have pulled the proverbial wool over the eyes of the credulous masses.

That said, if one were to break capitalism down into a cult-like entity, one could do so by noticing right away that capitalism forces workers to work until utter exhaustion. The entity that is capitalism and the corporations within capitalism do not have the capacity to "care" about how many hours people work in a day. If people work until physical collapse and exhaustion, which frequently does happen, no one ever rushes to the aid of the collapsed and overworked worker. It's simply written off as just part of life. People already work too many hours and are not able to spend quality time with their friends, family and other loved ones.

The workers in America are taught to adopt the protestant work ethic of hard work or no play. There's no play time until all the work is done. Many people work overtime hours and work on weekends. Many workers work during their "off time", during their evenings or in the middle of the night. Many people are "on call" and must respond to calls from their employers no matter when the calls come in. If it's at 3:00 am, well then – so be it. Much of this work is physical in nature – as in "manual labor" while a great deal of such work is done as "office work", dealing with answering emails, phone calls and doing certain tasks on computers and using smart phones. Law enforcement officers such as detectives and investigators and other first responders obviously have to be on call. Nurses and doctors too. That's sort of well known.

I'm thinking more specifically about ordinary office workers who end up working on "work" they bring home. Instead of sleeping or focusing on being present with their children, family members or friends, they put much of their focus in the work that they are "suppose" to leave behind *at work at the end of the work day*.

The second cult-like quality I see in capitalism is all the "gurus" and CEOs who're literally worshipped by society. CEOs such as Jeff Bezos or Warren Buffett or Bill Gates or the late Steve Jobs. The infamous Elon Musk is invariably worshipped as a "god of capitalism" because of his contributions to capitalism as a billionaire his status as a captain of industry. His invention of the Tesla electric car is his legacy. Vendor giant Amazon is Jeff Bezos's legacy as well. This is not necessarily a good thing or bad thing. These are simply facts that don't always need a moral-value judgment. Everyone shops at some point in time for *something* on Amazon *whether they want to or not*. It is a very strong powerhouse in the realm of capitalism. It's like Amazon is *the poster entity for the meaning of capitalism*.

When one views interviews by these "gurus of capitalism", one gets the feeling that these people are either your best friend or they're so far detached from ordinary (common people) that they might as well be living on another planet. The astonishing and remarkable amount of wealth these people have is beyond anything most of us can possibly fathom. These men are untouchable and thus, are the *messiahs of capitalism*. Many of them seem to literally have a narcissistic messiah complex (Donald Trump, for example). I'm not so sure that what I'm saying is hyperbole either. Trump has an obvious cult-like following and leadership within the political entity known as the G.O.P. Grand old party. Conservative republicans simply worship and adore everything he says and does. Some evangelical Christians believe Trump is the second coming of Christ himself! How this is not a red flag for professional theologians is beyond me.

Trump and his followers *could well* help him *usher in the age of American fascism with him as dictator* (i.e., cult leader). This (to me) is incredibly frightening. All I can hope for is that this never happens! Men with such power, can do (and do) some amazingly good things for society…but they can also do some profoundly disturbing things for society. Take your pick. Whatever whim they currently are obsessing on has both direct and indirect consequences for everyone.

Another way capitalism can be compared to cults is in how workers often have to uproot themselves and their families to move to other states in America where "the jobs are." If an industry packs up and leaves a given town or geological area, people often move away to follow the employers to wherever they decide to move company headquarters. Elon Musk moved from California to Texas in an attempt to cheat the tax system (i.e., make more profits with his business ventures). I'm sure that meant many of his employees and "followers" had to involuntarily uproot themselves and their families accordingly.

Often times, companies will even move their headquarters overseas to third-world nations in order to evade the IRS and all in attempts to avoid paying taxes. They move funds into offshore bank accounts that aren't bound to the rules and regulations of the American financial system. Wall Street bankers are considered "rock stars" and often act like "bad boy" rock stars in the way they live extraordinary lavish lifestyles. Luxurious excess is often their way of being (and *bling-ing,* LOL!).

It's nothing for ultra rich folks to spend multiple thousands of dollars on any given Friday or Saturday night while going out to eat and going to VIP dance clubs and other high profile locations where ultra wealthy people like to hang out. Ordinary people end up worshipping these "gods of big finance" and dream of going to college to study and major in "business" so they can "make lots of money" like the men on Wall Street and the captains of industry in capitalism. Meanwhile conservative republicans and other bad actors are stripping the liberal arts out of high schools, colleges and universities all across the country. Majoring in business becomes a sort of peer-pressured thing to do. Why major in a discipline that *doesn't* "make someone rich" or at least very well off (eventually)?

People end up getting brain washed into adopting certain work ethics and ideas about the pursuit of money in the "cult of capitalism." People end up thinking that money is a god-like entity in their lives. Many libertarians often end up behaving like literal sociopaths in their "Ayn Rand" pursuit of wealth and worship of the free market. One business owner I designed a website for many years ago here in San Diego was a *Milton Friedman* and "free market capitalist" guru. He constantly proselytized capitalism and the free market by holding workshops and hosting events where local libertarians of San Diego would meet and greet discussing the wonders of capitalism and "the free market." It was nauseating for me, but at the same time, I learned a great deal about Milton Friedman and libertarian political ideologies. The knowledge I gleaned from being around Jesse (*last name not included*) would help me in learning more in addition to what I'd read in *Naomi Klein's book The Shock Doctrine: The Rise of Disaster Capitalism.*" That's a great book, by the way. She discusses Milton Friedman and the "Chicago School". Klein wrote a scathing analysis of how that institution of higher education did its part in ushering in fascism in the South American country of Chile during the 1970's. Readers of this book might enjoy reading her book.

When I did some research about libertarians, I would

come to the conclusion (as some social scientists have) that libertarians (as well as many republicans) could essentially be loosely & colloquially diagnosed as "sociopaths and / or psychopaths" simply based on their callus and cold attitudes - and lack of remorse regarding poor people. They essentially have no remorse or empathy for the plight of poor folks. Their attitudes toward people who collect welfare, for example are devoid of loving, warm, compassionate or empathetic human emotions. Their attitude is that everyone (excluding them, of course) should simply "pull themselves up by their boot straps." They believe getting money from welfare or social safety nets is abominable. They think everyone should essentially fend for themselves with absolutely no help from the federal government.

Remember most republicans want *small government if any at all*. What they want certainly is *not* to offer financial aid to people who are having trouble putting gas in their cars or food on the table. In fact, many libertarians I know abhor the notion of there even being a federal government. Many of them are anti-government and extremely pro-capitalist. The socialist notions I've written about here are essentially blasphemous and I should have my mental health examined immediately (or worse). I can imagine just what toxic notions shall come to people's minds who read this book or see the title of this book who're polar opposites of where I am politically and socially. However, I'm ready for it. I'm a strong, formidable individual. I pride myself to a fault in being a far-left liberal. Let's just say I don't think too highly of libertarians or anyone who vehemently sides with people such as Donald Trump or Elon Musk. People who think there's nothing wrong with capitalism are my ideological and philosophical enemies. I know this. But I'm not afraid of this either. While I'd like to bridge the deep divide that has inevitably been created among Americans (politically and socially in many areas of culture and life), I'm not willing to allow the slithering snakes and reptiles of capitalism to poison me with their delusions of free market grandeur.

Another way to compare capitalism to cults is in sex and sex workers. The fact that so many women (and men) end up resorting to selling themselves for sex is problematic in the sense that so many people can't afford to make ends meet otherwise. They end up feeling that they "have" to work as sex workers and sell themselves in the traditionally capitalist way. There's obviously much I could write about this topic. Even if you ignore the problem of the illegal sex trade and sex trafficking of women and young girls, even more appropriate or "classy" forms of selling sex is still very much cult-like. Women and men end up being reduced to sex objects for millions and millions of horny and perverted men. Men are also sex objects for millions and millions of horny and perverted men. People sell their dirty / used underwear online, people sell used condoms, people even sell their own excrement and other "bodily fluids" online in an attempt to make customers happy. There's the explosion of the very famous website known as "Only Fans" that allows individuals to make money from their bodies. They can perform various sexual acts and antics in order for "fans" to get off and get their sexual needs met "for a fee" of course. Financial transactions are made just like on any other ecommerce website. It's no different than buying a book or coffee table online. Except in this case, customers are buying a sex show of sorts.

This sexual component isn't necessarily directly comparable in the way that cult gurus and leaders often demand sex from their inner circle cult members, but you can see that in capitalism, not even sex is off limits. Selling sex and the fact that "sex sells" is as old as capitalism itself. I am not unaware of this fact. It might be stretching it a bit to make such a comparison, but I think most readers reading this will at least give me a proverbial pass and say "okay" – if you say so! Unless I've really missed something, I can't think of too many more things to say about sex and capitalism in terms of the sexual component of cults. As I said before, there's already much that could be said about sex and capitalism in general and in other ways…but that's not the topic of this book. I want to stay focused on why I think capitalism should simply be stopped and destroyed at all costs. Keep in mind that this simple comparison is not at all complete and I've most likely missed many things I could have written much more order to make a more precise assessment of the issue. The bottom line is this: whether capitalism is a cult or not is not the main issue here. There are more reasons that I will write about in order to make the general argument that capitalism is inhumane and should be utterly destroyed. I personally think that any system that uproots individuals and families, works them until utter exhaustion and thrusts people into poverty is one that should be avoided and destroyed if, whenever & wherever possible. If the reasons I've listed don't make one see the comparison of capitalism to cults, then I don't know what could make readers see what I have seen. Regardless, I still think capitalism has many "cult-like" qualities that should make people pause and re-think what it means to let capitalism continue as it is currently being practiced. People are dying because *we humans aren't innovative enough* to destroy the current system and design a new system that allows humans to enjoy more freedoms and live more free lives!

Wrapping up, I will write in my next chapter about the notion of single individuals having billions of dollars. *Does anyone (single individual) actually deserve to have even a billion dollars let alone billions of them?* I personally don't think so. I know many other people feel the same way. Thus, I will make the argument that *no one* deserves to acquire that much money and personal wealth.

# Chapter 6: No one should possess a billion or more dollars

If I could come up with only one point to argue about why capitalism should be destroyed, it would be the notion of single individuals *not deserving to have billions of dollars* (personally). I believe it is an abomination for any single individual to possess a billion (*let alone billions*) of dollars. *I don't care what they've done or who they are. No one (in my mind) deserves billions of dollars!* Not even a single billion. Since I'm against money altogether and since I am vehemently anti-capitalist, I can't say what "amount" of "money" anyone should really have. In the past. I've said that it might be okay to have so many millions of dollars, but exactly how many? I understand single actors, musicians or artists who've *really worked hard* and *have made a difference and contribution in the world* to have a million dollars or even multi-millions of dollars. That much seems oaky. But when you get up to the level of a billion or more dollars.... How much is enough? I just haven't decided exactly how many millions I'm willing to cap if off at. All that is in assuming that our current system of capitalism cannot be destroyed; it's assuming that there's absolutely nothing that can be done to exterminate it or drastically transform it.

However, since I envision a different system – a completely different world, I feel awkward in even thinking about a maximum amount of money anyone should be able to possess as an individual. That's a very authoritarian and quite "fascistic" thing to say, actually. I know this. I mean, I wish we didn't even have to deal with this topic. Alas – we must. So then, I will discuss the reasons why I think no one should be socially and legally allowed to possess a billion or more dollars. *Why? For starters, no one ever actually earns a billion dollars single handedly.* It took hundreds or even thousands of other people (employees and others) to enable all the well-known and famous CEOs to earn their billions.

The entire U.S. economy is actually responsible for CEOs earning that much money. The ebbs and flows of the stock market come into play when determining what exactly will help to enable a single company earn so many millions and billions of dollars during each business cycle. Being that I'm no economist or financial expert, I'm not even sure if I'm using the correct language here. I'm not good at math either…so I'm not using anything but a very rudimentary level of thinking to conclude that NO ONE should be allowed to possess that kind of money.

If trillions & billions of dollars are going to continue exist in capitalism, then who or what should be able to manage, contain or possess that kind of wealth? *I think organizations should.* Nations, *(governments* and *single (or multiple) organizations* should be allowed to possess maintain and strictly regulate billions or more dollars. This would obviously apply to trillions of dollars as well.

Trillions of dollars are too dizzying of a concept for a single person to even think about, let alone handle. Such large amounts of money definitely have to be handled by multiple organizations. I almost fall through the floor when I contemplate exactly how much money many billionaires have access to. I know I would certainly fall through the floor if it really became a thing for trillionaires to exist. For the argument of this book, *I'm capping it off at a billion dollars, absolute maximum.* Anything above and beyond a billion dollars will be the exclusive property of certain corporations or governments of nations around the world.

At no point should a single individual be able to possess that much in wealth or assets. What will happen to an individual's funds at the point at which it accrues to a billion is beyond the scope of this chapter. If I had to hazard an imaginative guess here, I would say that banks and other governmental institutions should quickly and immediately take hold (seize) funds above and beyond the billion-dollar mark. Laws and rules would be enacted to give that money to appropriate institutions and the federal government. Exactly how this would be carried out is also beyond the scope of this book. My point is that it would be done automatically so that no one has to even think about it. A system could be set up that begins to direct funds away from sing individuals who earn that amount of money.

What I can say is that any organizations, governments and collective entities that would be allowed to possess billions or more dollars would be required (*again by law*) to *properly distribute* the extra billions of dollars into the national economy and directly to citizens who live within the countries in question.

For corporations who threaten to move overseas (from America, for instance), there will (or should be) *international laws put into place and enacted that prohibit corporations and wealthy individuals from any country from moving to other countries in order to exploit various loop holes and tax regulations.* Politicians talk a lot about taxes. Democrats talk about raising taxes and paying taxes.

Republicans love talking about cutting taxes and paying nothing in taxes. Some people want others to pay and others wish to pay nothing back to the communities that enabled them to become ultra rich and successful. Well, in my new system (or in a decently designed new system, evading taxes and such financial shenanigans would simply be prohibited. It just wouldn't be possible. But, that's assuming a new system that still uses "money." Ultimately, I would love to see a moneyless society. In subsequent chapters, I will discuss more about how goods and recourses could be distributed. Because that's what I really think this is about. *I'm really talking about a system of fair distribution.* We already live in "an era of abundance" – *why not use that abundance to spread goods to people who need them the most?* Factories and the machines that make the products and goods we all love *already exist* and can be *re-created to scale*

66

for demand. *We can simply continue to manufacture and distribute goods and services such that everyone has their most basic necessities distributed to them according to individual and personal need.*

Whenever I hear of billionaires, I think of homeless people. I think of myself and how much money I don't have. I think of what exact amount of money any one human being *needs* to have on a daily basis or annual basis. *Above and beyond a certain amount of money, we humans can't even compute the amounts of excess that billionaires have.* It's hard enough for me to imagine what I'd do with one million dollars, let alone many, many millions of dollars. *Beyond a certain point (beyond a certain amount of money) people don't need much money.* Existentially speaking, when people have their most basic needs met, money becomes just something extra. *The only thing is, it's well known that when people become richer, their "needs" and the things and services they "want" exponentially exceed what they initially imagined they needed or wanted.* This of course, ties back into the selfishness and greed problem I outlined in chapter 4.

Really, what I have always maintained, is that *until and unless there are absolutely no poor or homeless people existing on planet earth, there should never exist a billionaire.* As much as I love pop culture and admire certain highly innovative entrepreneurs, I still have a hard time thinking it's okay for many of them to be rich and wealthy.

Notice I didn't say rich and successful, because – just becoming famous and being innovative is successful enough in my humble opinion. I don't mind people like Madonna, Lady Gaga, Taylor Swift or Beyoncé getting insanely successful or even a bit rich from what they've done. Some people might even opine that even they didn't necessarily earn *all* of the money received in their cultural endeavors. Some celebrities and well-known entrepreneurs really do contribute more towards the common good and common people than many super / ultra rich people do. There are some exceptions. However, get this: all pop stars and well-known celebrities have had the financial backing of entire occupations and industries that are devoted to *ensuring* they would become the famous and noteworthy.

I understand talk like this is all in regards to the how things "should or ought" to work under the existing monetary capitalistic social structure. The current structure uses money as a means of exchange. The only thing is that *Money itself has become a thing to own, hoard and possess.* How to obtain money, how to maintain a sufficient flow of it and how to hoard it is everyone's business and the stuff of countless articles, magazines, books, videos, podcasts and movies. Money is even considered the "root of all evil" by spiritual and religious folks. Thus, the idea that any one man or woman should be proud to possess a billion or more dollars is often thought of by many middle-class, poor and homeless people as blasphemous and absurd. As an existentialist philosopher, I find it "utterly absurd" that people can amass such wealth. Such excess doesn't impress me. Who doesn't like nice things? Who doesn't or who wouldn't like living in the lap of luxury? The saying, "It must be nice!" (to have luxurious items) is a common thing to hear people say. Aside from whatever criminal dealings one may have done in his or her life, I believe that *every human being on earth deserves to live in the lap of luxury if they so choose.* The option should be made available to them, *simply because they exist.* That is, of course – all according to the actual amount of physical recourses we're able to extract from the Earth in a sustainable manner to make such accoutrements a reality.

If we're not able to adapt successfully to the changes in our climate because of *already existing climate changes*, a future moneyless system using nothing but Earth's resources and synthetic (human made) resources will be much more challenging to create. I'm already under the impression that we've extracted all that we can from the Earth. Beyond what is considered "normal", "good" or "enough", we've done nothing but damage the very planet that gives us life.

I love life enough to constantly be imagining a world where we didn't have to use or have "money" to exist. When I look at birds and other animals, I think of how much more freedom those beings have than we do as humans. Money and capitalism aside, our world of religion, politics and war is enough to make one go insane. However, we humans do exist alongside the animals in the animal kingdom. Not a single one of them (no other primate) has what we have created with this thing called capitalism. Capital...money...exchanging bits of paper or having hallucinatory digital commerce dealings done on computers is a uniquely human phenomenon. At any rate American society (and other countries' citizens) should really begin thinking about how to transition from a money and class system to a classless system that actually embraces human freedom and dignity. Being that we currently have to contend with cash money, we should be using our collective imagination to bring forth the next economic evolution and "revolution." I've always considered myself sort of a visionary. I've always had an over-active imagination. I guess that what drew me to art, web & graphic design in previous phases of my life.

# Chapter 7: Capitalism Causes Many Crimes

It is my personal opinion that capitalism is the cause of an awful lot of crimes that are committed. Many white collar and violent crimes can be traced back to capitalism in some way. This is never discussed by the mainstream media because that would disrupt the business-as-usual system of advertising. It's a sort of "elephant in the room" situation where it's not spoken out loud, but everyone sort of knows it's an "unspoken" phenomenon. People in financial distress have been shown to do extremely dangerous and violent things in order to maintain their lifestyles and ways of living.

It doesn't take seasoned police detectives or prosecutors to tell us that many people hire "hitmen" to murder & kill others who're prove to be an obstacle in their capitalistic (materialistic) way of living. We see it all the time on display in television drama shows, reality true crime shows and in news headlines each evening. The saying that money is the root of all evil points to the crimes that people commit in the pursuit of maintaining lavish lifestyles and ways of being. Because of people's addictive tendencies to various things and activities, many violent crimes are carried out when certain obstacles arise and prevent the normal processes of capitalism to take place.

How many times do we see true crime shows explaining the motives behind certain murders? It's too common to

71

ignore. When people act surprised to discover that money was somehow tied into a murderous plot it points to the fact that many times people don't see the most obvious things staring directly in their faces. You've probably heard the cliché "follow the money." Well, when you follow the money trail in certain crimes that have been committed, it becomes clear that people's need for selfishness and greed often gets the best of them and they end up killing others.

Even when money is not a direct motive in the commission of certain crimes, there's often still some way that one could make the case that the way people live their lives often causes them to have mental breakdowns and do things they wouldn't ordinarily do. I'm not naïve enough to suggest that capitalism is involved in every criminal case. I'm simply saying that it all-to-often is. In stretching this explanation out even further, one could even ask the question "Could it be that if people didn't have to run around like crazy 40 or 60 hours every week in the pursuit of meeting their most basic needs, that they might (just might) NOT be so angry and willing to partake in mischievous, dangerous or criminal acts? Even nonviolent crimes such as certain drug-related offenses exist only because in one way or another, people were simply trying to get certain physical and psychological needs met. However, in doing so, they get ensnared in the Prison-Industrial-Jim Crow-Complex which disproportionately punishes Blacks & Hispanics. White supremacist laws and governmental policies that have long been put into place cause the never-ending cycle of violence and unnecessary imprisonment of people in this craven and repugnant system of free market capitalism. The rules and dictates of capitalism (it seems) were designed by scrupulous people (mostly men) with many personal vices and antisocial tendencies. But this is seldom discussed because to even question the status quo of capital and capitalism is blasphemous and taboo.

The money trail of the prison system and legal system is too profitable for many people to have an initiative to stop. There are too many people being made fabulously wealthy by maintaining such a cruel penial system that punishes people for offenses that are truly nonviolent. Maintaining this status quo has been put on automatic default and no journalist in the American media ever seems to discuss this. Even when people are aware that capitalism is the problem, when you argue for socialism or Marxism, people often get indignant and defensive. Cognitive dissonance often results. Discussions of how to come up with a better system and way of living gets lost in the process. People proverbially plug their ears or dig their heals into the ground as if being dragged into a discussion they just can't handle. Pejorative terms such as communist and misconstrued concepts get tossed about. People end up misunderstanding the finer points of points being made by people on both sides of the debate.

There are obviously people who honestly and in good faith believe in the capitalist system because it has brought them and their families either out of poverty or into a much better standard of living. The talk of making money obsolete or destroying a system that has made them phenomenally wealthy is anathema. People often think that what works for them works for others (or should work for others). That's often not the case. One-size often does *not* fit all. There are concepts, situations and issues where it's very much not a zero-sum game. People's tempestuous beliefs regarding competition and cooperation also prevents them from being willing to envision or participate in situations that don't use money and capitalistic dealings.

In getting back to discussing how capitalism promotes and causes many criminal elements within society, I'll say that the very much capitalistic war on drugs created a booming business of the underground drug trade. Movies, television shows and documentaries fill the streaming platforms with all the organization, violence and mayhem that has been caused in the history of the infamous war on drugs. It's like one form of crony capitalism being against another form of crony capitalism and business dealings. As existentialist philosophers might proclaim – "the war on drugs was and is definitely absurd."

# Chapter 8: The Cheapness of Capitalism

I have always been amazed and quite fascinated with how "cheap" things made and bought within a capitalistic system are. I've always had a nagging feeling inside my mind that whenever I bought something, no matter how expensive, there was always something about it that felt kind of cheap. The relative cheapness of capitalism can also be felt when you feel that you're not getting what you really should (or deserve to get) when you purchase a certain product. I think many consumers are aware that companies tend to cut as many corners as they can when creating and distributing products because after all, "everything revolves around profits." Whatever manufactures can do to "cut costs" and "lower prices" of certain items ends up becoming part of the calculus that workers within given industries must pay attention to.

Everyone has heard the saying "You get what you pay for." While this is largely true in many areas of capitalism, it's not always true in many other areas of what I will call "the-supposedly-free-but-nothing-is-really-free-market." Sometimes consumers who pay more for given products and services end up with quite a bit less than other consumers who purchased the same product and type of service from a different vendor. In doing my research into self-publishing, etc., I've seen the exact same service being offered for free and simultaneously being sold for an exorbitant amount of money by another company. The cliché of "you get what you pay for" could be true in some cases, but it can also be absolutely false in other cases where unwitting consumers get sucked into the overall "scam" of capitalism. People can often purchase the exact same thing for a far lower price or even for free while other consumers end up giving away their hard-earned money in questionable and nefarious commerce dealings. People get ripped off all the time. It's a shame. But it happens all too often. This is all part of what I am calling the "cheapness" of capitalism.

Companies and corporations pay huge amounts of money for ad campaigns that try to get consumers' attention. We're told that if only we had "this product" or partake in that service that our lives would somehow be enhanced. Even if such words are never mentioned in marketing dialogue, the feelings and emotions end up being the end result. People feel they have to purchase certain items in order to show their status and wealth in society. They do this also to show that they are "in the know" and "fashionable" and so on. Marketing hype is quite psychological and preys on consumers' trust and vulnerabilities. Get people hooked on various practices and things (like smoking and vaping) and billion dollar industries are created in an instant. Marketers know just how to get into the heads of consumers. Tell them what they want to hear or tell them how they can be more successful and you've got them. They'll be partial to whatever "brand" or company is telling them how to look good, feel good and be successful in life.

Other ways the cheapness of capitalism reveals itself is when you open a product like say, a new iPhone and there's something about the "experience" that seems…chincy. For instance, Apple is a company that prides itself on its minimalistic approach to design and packaging. That's fine both for environmental and even artistic reasons. However, the utter simplicity of opening new consumer devices often left me feeling very underwhelmed. I felt like I spent hundreds of dollars for what? Oh, yeah – "this." iPhones and other consumer electronic devices often do convey a feeling of cheapness that people generally don't expect. Perhaps that's just people having too many expectations in what they buy. But when you're paying hundreds or even many thousands of dollars for some - (thing), you'd expect the experience of opening, feeling and see it for the first time to live up to high standards and expectations. There's nothing wrong with that.

Asking for truly robust and high quality products at reasonable prices is shouldn't be seen as an insult by CEO's and others who run morbidly rich corporations. Consumers are not asking for something impractical. Asking for what one deserves for spending their often hard-earned money should never be looked at as a bad thing. To defend Apple, I will say that all of the products I've ever bought have been quite stellar and extremely robust in terms of quality. I can't always say that about other products I've purchased in the past from other well-known corporations.

Electronics and other often-used items shouldn't have such short self-lives. Planned obsolescence shouldn't be a thing either. I understand profits will (unfortunately) always be king in repugnant and rapacious capitalism, but the bold, daring and most honorable thing for any company to do is to resist the profits-at-all-costs mentality and actually produce the best quality and most affordable product possible for consumers.

When you really think about it, it's us (the consumers) who ultimately decide whether corporations live or die! That last sentence is tongue-in-cheek talk making fun of the pathetic notion that corporations are people. Supreme Court take notice! Your landmark decision which ruled that corporations are people is *exactly what makes people in America and countries all over the world lose all faith in institutions* that have been around for millennia.

In my next chapter I will talk about the very common, but very tragic concept of people being evicted from their homes. I'm warning morbidly rich people who read this that – the American people will eventually be coming for you. Whether it's through physical violence or by simple political legislation is entirely up to you. I don't condone violence, but when push comes to shove, something's got to give. Being morbidly rich can only keep a crumbling empire alive for so long.

# Chapter 9: The Trauma of Being Evicted

One of the most terrifying things imaginable for me is to be evicted from my home. Not my apartment. Not my house. My home. See, my tiny one-bedroom apartment that I share with my domestic partner (my husband: I'm not married) is my home. We've all heard the very cliché-but-true saying "home is where the heart is." For many billions of people on planet Earth, home truly is where their proverbial hearts exist. Their spirit – their essence exists in a home that is not only shelter from the storm – it's their sanctuary. It's the very place where they can be themselves, free of judgments and abuse from the outside world. In decent and wholesome homes where physical, sexual and emotional abuse does not occur, people are their own-most unique selves when concealed in the privacy of that home.

However, capitalism comes in with its vile and predatory dictates and utterly ejects people from their homes all because…all because they did not pay the stupid rent on time. Oh, maybe it has been added up and become many months or even (in some cases) years where tenants have not been able to produce the funds required to pay the debt of rent. Something very bad happens in people's lives. A dishonorable and very tragic thing happens on a daily basis in America and other countries around the world: People…get…evicted.

79

A very reputable and honest author **Matthew Desmond** published a book in 2017 titled *Evicted: Poverty and Profit in the American City*. If I remember correctly, in it – he wrote about his experiences living as a renter in mobile home (trailer parks). He wrote about the physical and mental trauma that human beings face when they're thrust from their living domains. Local sheriffs and other law-enforcement officers storm in like storm troopers and violently pound loudly on tenants' doors knowing that many of them might be trying to hide or pretend not to be home so as to not dare answer the door. Some tenants become "squatters" which makes landlords' jobs more difficult by having to go to court multiple times to pay for these sheriff departments to serve multiple eviction notices.

The whole process of eviction uproots people from their daily routines and prevents them from being able to take steps necessary to get themselves into better financial positions. Not everyone has friends or family members they can stay with. Nor do they have the money to temporarily stay in hotel or motel rooms. Single people living alone who've been put in the position of being evicted either by things they've done in their personal lives or by external (capitalistic) forces, often don't have anyone to turn to for financial or physical help. In many cases, people become homeless. In many cases, people who've been sober for decades say "fuck it" and begin using what money they do have left to consume alcohol and other drugs. Some people being to turn to carrying out petty crimes because they've been recently evicted. They'll do whatever they "have" to do in order to cope with and deal with the reprehensible fact of having been ejected out of their sanctuaries.

Morbidly rich people cannot and do not put themselves in the proverbial shoes of evicted individuals because they live in such a detached mental and physical world where they don't have to experience such hardships. So they forget what it's like or never ever even know what it's like for a person to become homeless. Rich people (and even many middle-class people) often mock and ridicule the poor and homeless people in an attempt to make themselves feel good. They think that because they've obtained or (less frequently) actually worked for the multi-millions or many thousands of dollars they possess somehow makes them "above" and "better" than the poor and dispossessed.

It is a known fact that when people become rich, they forget what it was like to be poor. They lose the psychological emotional capacity to empathize with poor people and thus become numb, apathetic and indifferent to the plights of the poor. Dispossessed people may as well not even exist in the minds of most middle-class and wealthy people.

Being evicted strips people of their very humanity. It perverts their entire being. It cleaves their identities. Being evicted is something many people are embarrassed about. The fact that banks and other financial institutions regard being evicted as a bad thing or "mark" against them is absolutely disgusting in my philosophical and personal opinion. Whatever happened to some things being held as sacred? I think things like one's sanctuary and sense of home is sacred and should not be touched by the dictates and whims of the economy and predatory capitalism. The "people" (*corporations*) behave in atrociously predatory ways when sending armed and extremely physically intimidating men to people's apartments and houses in order to serve arbitrary eviction notices.

Being evicted is an indignity that no one should ever have to experience. The fact that most morbidly rich people (or even generally rich people) will never face being thrust or ejected from their sanctuaries is something poor and homeless people just do not understand. Ever since I became close to homelessness a few short years ago, I feel like I've been scarred for life. I will never feel normal or okay inside. I will never feel like I "have" anything or that I live anywhere. I've been traumatized by capitalism and the evictors. I've seen people get evicted from their homes. I've seen news reports of people being slaughtered by the police officers who stormed to their apartments to serve eviction papers. It frightens me. I cried recently from seeing neighbors I grew to like quite a bit be ousted like sheep from their sleeping dens. I just can't see how human beings can be so cruel. ***But capitalists do***. In a very real but maybe indirect way, it can be said that all capitalists love such cruelty. In fact, I dare say many of them (like Donald Trump) *thrive* on it. ***After all, it's all just another day's work....***

82

# Chapter 10: Possible Alternatives to Capitalism

Universal basic income is one possible way to transition into the kind of society that I envision for the future. Universal basic income might seem like a novel concept to many readers, but it's really not so new. Historical civil rights activist and leader Martin Luther King Jr. was an early proponent of UBI. The basic idea is that if people receive a guaranteed income each month of about one to two thousand dollars (or more) per month (to cover their most basic needs), they'll then begin using the extra money to better themselves and their families. People might start a new business or renovate their homes, help other people financially and other things. Also, that extra money gets spent in the actual American economy each day. Once people feel less financial pressure in their life, they can breathe easier and begin to live better (less self-destructive) lives. Former democratic presidential nominee Andrew Yang ran for president using UBI as his big selling point.

UBI is a kind of socialism as well. All socialism really is – is everyone gets treated equally, in a business setting, workers get to decide what is done with all the profits of the organization or business. In a socialist business structure, there is no one "CEO" at the top or "shareholders" who get to hoard all the profits of the company. All persons involved in the company get to decide what happens with profits made

84

by the work that they previously performed. It's as simple as that. Socialism is not communism (communism is really only a more extreme form of socialism). It's not atheism either. In other words: it's not the boogieman that conservatives, republicans, libertarians or politically independent people want you to think it is. A lot of people don't really understand what socialism even is. So when they hear that someone is going to receive money from the government, they cry foul and say people shouldn't receive "handouts." What? You mean your very own government is not meant to ever help you? Are you sure about that? Think more closely before judging harshly what the government should or should not be allowed and able to do. Conservatives would probably love to take advantage of government handouts so long as it benefits them and their families. They don't want the democrats and their families to experience the same thing. Republicans have a double standard when discussing social welfare and what the government should do to help those who're less financially fortunate.

The precise alternatives to capitalism could possibly take form in a wide variety of ways. Society could institute a universal basic income and then slowly transition away from using money altogether but still have a universal means of distribution for the goods and services that people really need. A transition will likely take place, as such a complicated system will need some amount of time to come into fruition. I'm not a politician or engineer, so I can't authoritatively predict what could or is likely to happen. All I know is this: a monumental and drastic change must take place. The planet is dying. Populations of animals and plants are becoming extinct because of our capitalistic (negatively selfish) ways of existing.

As I've said before, I am not naïve. I am not someone who entertains ideas of utopia & pipe dreams where everyone suddenly loves each other in tranquil harmony. Though that would be very nice, I know it's just not realistic. *What is realistic* is *that we are very capable of coming up with a new system of mass-distribution*. Distributing physical necessities humans need to survive is possible *right now* because we are living in what many thinkers have dubbed the "era of abundance." It is in this abundance that we can create a new kind of socialism – one that works very well. It's already been demonstrated how small-scale socialist environments can work. If the workers in a small bakery in San Francisco can create a well-oiled shop that produces pastries, the template can be scaled up to accommodate a much larger amount of workers and communities. Politicians and diplomatic individuals can establish new laws that incentivize people to behave in the new ways of being (according whatever the new system or "ism" ends up being). *Living in peace and harmony on planet Earth doesn't have to be just a John Lennon song "Imagine" concept.* It's only a pipe dream if we continue to allow hopeless-bleak-despair-capitalism to continue perverting what it means to be a human being.

85

Speaking of socialism – I can't stand it when opponents of socialism inevitably begin listing all the historical examples where socialism (and communism) have failed. Sure, if you install fascist dictators into nations and force everyone all at once to begin living in ways they're not accustomed to, then sure – that form of "ism" will not work. Keeping in mind that I'm no historian (I'm unemployed and possess only two years of college), but I do know that it doesn't take rocket science to think about some of the details of what a new economic system might look like. Living in a moneyless society can be incredibly enlightening and dare I say "spiritually uplifting?" I believe it can be. I'm certainly not spiritual or religious (*I'm an atheistic existentialist*).

A new society can take the good parts of socialism and craft a new political and economic system that incorporates true human freedom into the equations that end up becoming part of the process of that new system. I use the word *system* because that's what it'll be. Many brilliant people are already envisioning a new system of commodity distribution where there will be no numerical digital hallucination transactions taking place over the internet. New databases and computing systems will exist that keep track of the physical manufacturing and distribution of everything humans need and use in their daily lives, period. Free will be the new way. Free will be the best way. The economy could be a free economy of sorts. All things being free will become a very cherished and protected way of life. Even psychopaths and narcissists will appreciate their new freedoms. I say that because I'm also not naïve enough to think that destroying capitalism will be the solution to all of humanities woes. Of course it won't. However, I'm willing to wager that a free system could possibly decrease the amount of physical & mental violence that takes place within the world. How much is anyone's guess. Since no one can predict exactly what the changes will be, it's not really prudent to waste much time on discussing what could (or could not) end up being the case.

When I think of all the possible solutions to our current system of predatory repugnant capitalism, I'm really struck that we're not already trying this in America on a large scale. People often talk about taming capitalism or making it "better", which in my eyes is just a mediocre way of thinking. We can do better than keeping money in any form. *We can abolish it altogether.* It *doesn't have to be so complicated.* But…I don't really have too much faith in humanity doing what should be done. We've already seen too many instances in history where what should have been done or what could have been done was simply never done. In many cases, the exact opposite of what could or should have been done was implemented and carried out in often horrific ways. The philosophical nihilist and pessimist in me says humans will continue to shoot themselves in their feet. But the small but ever-so-strong optimist in me does actually believe that humanity will see better days in the future. Many things may seem hopelessly bleak and miserable now, but hopeless-bleak-despair doesn't have to be the only mood of men.

Side note: I use the term hopeless-bleak-despair in sentences in this dialogue to salute my favorite alternative rock band on planet Earth: *They Might Be Giants* (mentioned earlier in chapter 1). TMBG wrote a song in one of their famous albums titled *Hopeless Bleak Despair,* in their September 11th, 2001 released album, *Mink Car.* Pop music and playful fun aside, we're fully capable of ushering in a bright new way of being in the world. *At least that's what I really want to believe.* If one wishes to regard such thoughts as mere utopian pipe dreams, well then – so be it.

I'll leave the exact solutions for people smarter than me to posit and speculate about. I'm certainly not the only author who has theorized possible solutions. On a personal level, I've been thinking about these issues for many years. As someone who is relatively well read, it shouldn't take a linguist or philosopher of language to put into words just what an alternative to capitalism could really be. People such as author Mathew Holten suggest that society simply needs to give citizens their most basic necessities (whatever they end up being). Create a comprehensive list of what such daily necessities are required in different communities all over the world. Variation will obviously exist as each person has different physical and mental health and other needs. Everything from kitchen and food preparation to what they need in their bathrooms and bedrooms to what they'll ultimately need in terms of healthcare. Everything. Craft a list of these things which will obviously vary from person to person and family to family. But…. It will be society's duty to fully implement and ensure that all items are manufactured and distributed in a way that gets to people in a timely and safe fashion. The controversial new technology known as AI (artificial intelligence) could even be used to keep create and maintain such logistical databases. Able-bodied people will be encouraged to work up until a certain age. Whether it's manual labor or white-collar work, *people will get to choose just what specific jobs they'd "like" to perform.* No one will be forced or coerced into doing things they don't wish to do. Their psychological needs for intrinsic and extrinsic rewards will be met even in free labor. What a great feeling it will be for people to know that the very work they're doing no matter how mundane, is helping everyone in community and world. In situations and places where needs aren't being met, teams of professionals will swoop in to ensure that individuals' needs begin to get met in a sufficient and safe manner. Again, AI and professional humans can monitor areas of the world where specific needs and goals are not being met and decide which action and strategic events need to take place.

Again, I'm not naïve. I know that for whatever unforeseen reasons, there will be people who inevitably fall through some unforeseen proverbial cracks in such a new system. No human system is fool proof. Any form of socialism is not without its problems just as any and all forms of capitalism will not be without similar problems.

89

***Just because we haven't seen many massive large-scale systems of socialism in action doesn't mean it cannot be achieved.*** I'm not willing to give up. Just because current capitalists claim and want readers to believe that capitalism is the only viable economic system or way of being in the world, that *does not mean that it is*…. That's like saying VHS cassette tapes were the only ways of viewing video content. How ridiculous that would have been. I think many readers probably have never even handled a VHS cassette video tape in their entire lives. My point is that capitalism surely isn't and certainly *doesn't have* to be the only way humans can get their most basic needs met. People have already published and are currently writing books that explain many of the aforementioned ideas that I've put forth in this publication. I just have to ask readers how badly they want change in society. For instance, we already know that memes evolve at an extremely rapid rate. Why not accelerate the rate of evolution in this case? Why not come together to not only save our dying democracies around the world, but *exterminate fascism* and catastrophic climate change altogether by ***re-thinking*** our daily existence?

If I had all the answers – well, I wouldn't be writing this book. The problem is that corrupt people are often drawn to power and end up keeping that power. It's rather unfortunate that politicians like to hold onto their power for decades without stepping down (Ruth Bader Ginsburg). Because American politics and American democracy is such a fragile entity, it's all too unclear and it seems very unlikely that

90

what I'm proposing will ever come into existence. I don't want this to be the case. That's why I think voting and being politically aware is vital in any democracy. Whether it's two parties or three or more, I say that it's incumbent upon every U.S. citizen to vote strategically to ensure their voices get heard in local and national elections. I understand many readers may have much disdain for the two party system in America. But right now that's all we have. I vote democrat for strategic reasons. I always vote democratic because it IS certainly better than voting any other way. Voting as a green party member is beyond me. One may as well give their votes to the republican party. I know, I know – I've heard all the arguments green party voters give for voting for politicians such as Ralph Nader (whom I don't have any problems with). I just think that liberals should be more strategic and use their vote in smarter ways. We can't afford to be making political statements by holding onto our specific philosophical and political principles. Sometimes one has to do *something even when and if it's considered socially and morally wrong.*

This political discussion compels me to mention that I used to have a tremendous amount of respect for public intellectual Cornel West. I've literally worshipped the philosopher for many years, but this year I've become utterly enraged at him. Why? He's "pulling a Ralph Nader." *He's running for president!* I've not kept up with all the specifics about it, but I have heard him state his case in interviews. While I may understand his philosophical and political

91

reasons for doing so and while I may agree with them – I don't think it's in America's best interest for him to do so. Quite the contrary. He should never have stepped into the political arena. I always thought men of his intellectual and moral caliber were far above stooping to the level of running for public office. I guess I was wrong. I think his legacy will somehow be tarnished because of this. I will always love Dr. West, but I don't think I can forgive him any time soon if (or god forbid when) his running for president ends up essentially giving the presidential election results to the dictator wannabe (Donald J. Trump). No – we Americans and people of the world MUST come up with a new system. We must find some way possible (quickly) to come up with a better system than capitalism once and for all.

# Chapter 11: The Absurdity of Sales Commercials

It has always been abundantly clear to me that sales ads and commercials are essentially...stupid and silly. Public service announcement ads aside, I've always thought traditional advertisements (and jingles) were just stupid and silly despite the alleged fact that billions of dollars have been made from various ad campaigns throughout the history of capitalist sales pitches. The notion that we're supposed to sit there and endure several minutes of interruption has always bothered me and I'm quite sure millions of others. It's no wonder that capitalists have exploited people's disdain for such nonsense by implementing paid tiers of services and packages on streaming platforms like YouTube, Hulu & Netflix that offer an ad-free experience.

Not everyone has the funds to spend on ensuring their minds aren't assaulted with *electronic hallucinations* (using author Chris Hedges's words again). Psychologists on both sides of the ad equation understand that people can only cope with so much information overload before they reach their alleged tipping point and begin getting frustrated and irritated by having to sit through and experience the onslaught of visual interruptions when the only thing they're trying to do is learn something or enjoy themselves by watching video content on the Internet or television screens. Anyone ever been to the Big Apple NYC (New York City)

93

Time's Square? I have…and as anyone who walks, drives through or rides through the world's advertising mecca knows just how psychologically "trippy" it is. However, it's an experience in and of itself that tourists all over the world either enjoy or are extremely underwhelmed with. In my head I thought, "Wow, what a vast area of visual distractions…."

New York's Times Square contains an incredible amount of physical & visual real-estate that's being used to gain the distracted attention of millions of people 24 hours a day, seven days a week. When I visited the city in December of 2003 for a week, I was utterly amazed at just how intense I thought it all was. However, residents who live near Time's Square must have gotten used to such visual and audible noise pollution and have maybe found ways to cope with and endure it whenever they go through that area. I guess that's what drives sales and people really do believe that advertising products and services to people really does work. I know ads *do* the job of getting people to remember to utilize certain brands and companies' offerings but how much mental abuse must we continue to take? Ads not only get me to purchase various products and services, but I find myself irritated, confused and depressed by them.

One way I cope with the visual onslaught of disrupting video ads is to close my eyes and ears (or mute the audio / skip ads) while at the same time zoning-out so I don't have to suffer so much mental abuse by capitalism's *insane universe of fake-pretend.* Why should social influencers on social media and authors trying to make a living by writing constantly have to be subjected to ***"prostituting themselves for the pimps of capitalism"?*** I would have thought marketing geniuses would have figured out a new way to monetize the whole thing by now. It's all just a bunch of manufactured BS if you ask me. The idea that Betty White and other celebrities have to brand themselves by showing up in capitalism ads is...kind of sad. Maybe it's just me. Or maybe it's just.... You get the point! People have made fortunes and livings by appearing in commercials that rake in billions of dollars for corporations around the world. On the one hand, it is kind of genius, but on the other hand, it's so silly and existentially absurd.

# Final Thoughts

I hope I've offered some account of what can or should be done to usher in a new way of being in the world. I know I'm not the only person who thinks this way. This work is just an introductory experience for people interested in the anti-capitalist / anti-capitalism & moneyless society movements. It's also my way of discussing and defining socialism. I hope I've made it clear to readers that socialism can definitely be something that is sustainable and robust. Socialism doesn't have to come in the form of dictatorships, commune cults, authoritarian regimes or anything else negative that we've been taught about in school and on television. The new way forward doesn't have to be any more or less complicated than we humans make it.

As a nation, *Americans are some of the most depressed and anxious people on Earth.* People are angry, irritable and many people have simply zoned out and have tried to live "off the grid." Many people have turned to drug and alcohol abuse as a result of living in such a hyper-capitalistic world. It's understandable why people want to give up their devices and just live as money-less as possible. *Life surely is strange.* My husband and I always say to each other, *"What a strange planet!" We truly do live in a toxic, traumatic & chaotic environments.* We've all made things this way by accepting things as they are. Read about all this and more in **Doctor Gabor Mate's** books. Mate writes about America's toxic culture in his book titled ***The Myth of Normal: Trauma, Illness and Healing in a Toxic Culture.***

I don't want to end my short book on a depressing note. Please keep in mind and think about all the things you can do in your daily lives to resist capitalism's narcissistic abuse. Just pause, take time out. Go on a walk. Be absorbed within nature. *Be present without devices and screens with your friends and family. Look each other in the eye and just "be with" whomever and whatever it is you wish to be with.* Maybe your dogs and cats can teach you a lot about life without capitalistic jingles and dingles. Learn a new hobby. Do something different that makes you happy and that doesn't involve money. Whatever works best for you is fine with me so long you don't hurt yourself or anyone else in the process. We all deserve a break. A huge…big…and tranquil break from the insanity and madness of capitalism and mundane commerce dealings. Thanks for reading my book! Be well….

# Previous Books by Shawn Gillick

**As a self-published / Indie author, I have five additional books currently available on Amazon.com** and other websites where books are sold in "print-on-demand" format. The titles and a brief description of ALL of my books follows below:

**NOTE: eBook readers** can simply *click on the book covers below* in order to purchase copies. If you have problems following the links, simply search for my first and last name **"Shawn Gillick"** in the *books* section of the **Amazon.com** website.

*New Existentialism: A Philosophy for the 21ˢᵗ Century*. This book is about the philosophy of existentialism and how it can be applied to modern life. I briefly touch on issues such as fascism, politics, religion, death and much more.

***Destroy Capitalism Before It Destroys Us!***
This book is about the negative and ill effects of capitalism and offers and alternative revolutionary economic system where money IS NOT used as the means of exchange. I discuss the concept of living in a "money-less" society.

## *Do Ask, Do Tell, Say Gay! A Memoir & Commentary On Being Gay in the United States Marine Corps.*

***This is about my time in the United States military*** during the **DADT (Don't Ask, Don't Tell)** ban on gay and lesbian military service.

*Work Equals Slavery: Why The Modern Workplace is a Form of Slavery*
**If you've ever wondered why it is so difficult to get a job, then this book is for you.** Possible solutions are presented alongside plenty of examples and philosophical analysis.

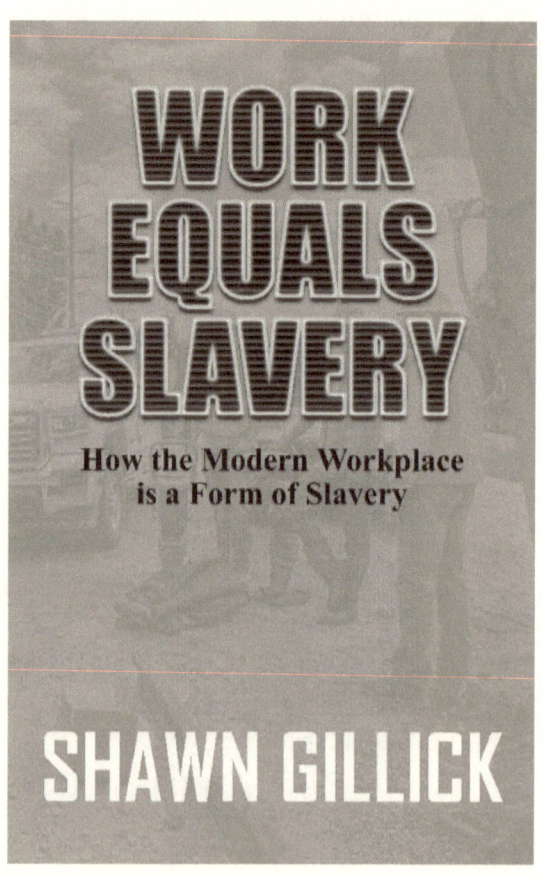

## *Beware of the Cult: How Cults Destroy Lives and How You Can Escape*

**In a world filled with so much political and spiritual uncertainty,** people are searching for meaning in their lives and often end up becoming involved with cults or "cult like" groups. *Shawn believes that essentially any group can become a cult.*

**Against a backdrop of rising authoritarianism, runaway corporate power, accelerating automation, and a climate in crisis,** *10 Steps to a Moneyless World* offers a clear, urgent roadmap for a radically different economic future where money is NOT used as a means of exchange.

**About me:** I'm *Shawn Gillick*, a former **U.S. Marine** who served during the **DADT (Don't Ask, Don't Tell) ban on gay and lesbian military service.**

> *I have also worked* as a freelance *web designer, graphic designer* and I am *extremely passionate* about *psychology* and *philosophy.* I keep up-to-date with both disciplines. I live here in beautiful (and often Sunny) San Diego, California.

*Scan QR Code with Smartphone Camera to view my Amazon.com author page!*